JESUS AND ME
IN THE SUMMER

BY JENNIE TODD

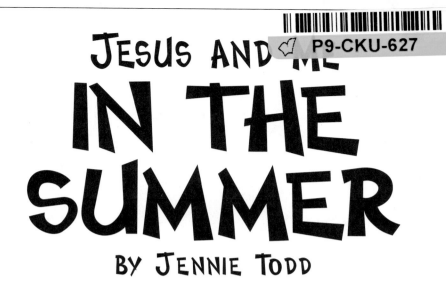

DEVOTIONS AND ACTIVITIES FOR TINY CHRISTIANS

Pacific Press Publishing Association
Boise, Idaho
Oshawa, Ontario, Canada

Edited by Jerry D. Thomas
Designed by Dennis Ferree
Cover and inside art by Consuelo Udave
Typeset in 14/20 Janson

Copyright © 1995 by
Pacific Press Publishing Association
Printed in the United States of America
All Rights Reserved

Library of Congress Cataloging-in-Publication Data

Todd, Jennie, 1959-
  Jesus and me in the summer : devotions and activities for tiny
Christians / Jennie Todd.
      p.   cm.
  ISBN 0-8163-1228-1
  1. Christian education of preschool children. 2. Preschool
children—Religious life.   I. Title.
BV1590.T63   1995
242'.62—dc20   94-2614
                                                              CIP

95 96 97 98 99 • 5 4 3 2 1

Contents

Jesus and Me . . .

Jesus and Me . . .
At Breakfast

"Give us, Lord, our daily bread," Kelly prayed. "Amen."

She opened her eyes. "Our bread really came from Acme, not the Lord. Mommy and I bought it."

Daddy nodded. "But where did Acme get the bread?"

"A bread truck!" Brad said. He made a roaring noise and pretended his bread was a truck driving around his plate.

"Where was the bread before it got on the truck?" Daddy asked him. Brad didn't answer. He was busy parking the bread beside his napkin.

"Maybe the truck got it from a bakery," Kelly said.

"Where would a bakery get bread?" Daddy asked.

"They made it with flour," Kelly answered, "like Grandma does."

"Flour is made from wheat," Daddy said. "And wheat grows from seeds . . ."

"And God makes seeds!" Kelly interrupted. "The Lord really does give us our daily bread!"

Bunnies, tigers, kangaroos,

Kittens, mice, and cockapoos;

Books, yo-yos, kites that fly,

Peanuts, raisins, Dad's new tie;

Dandelions, spider plants,

Dresses, socks, a pair of pants;

You give us, Lord, our daily bread,

Plus all those things that I've just said.

ACTIVITY
Making Butter

You Need: 1/2 pint whipping cream at room temperature, jar with screw on lid, crackers

Take turns shaking the cream until a lump of butter appears. Rinse and salt lightly. Spread on crackers to taste.

Use the time to talk about how God provides other things around the house (cotton clothes, books, etc.). Remember that your income, used to purchase items, is also a provision from God.

God Provides

Jesus and Me . . .
And the New Friend

Up. Back. Up. Back. Creak. Creak. Up. Back.

Jennifer moved her legs in the rhythm of the swing. "Higher, Daddy," she called over her shoulder.

Up. Back. Up. Back. Creak. Creak. Up. Back.

On the other side of the wall, she saw a girl about her age. Each time she went up, she got another peek.

Up—The girl had blond, curly hair—back.

Up—She hugged a doll—back.

Up—She wore shorts with pink polka dots—back.

Up—What was that?—back.

"Higher, Daddy," Jennifer asked. "Please."

Up—Jennifer's neighbor helped the girl into a metal chair with wheels—back.

Jennifer dragged her feet. The swing stopped in a cloud of dust. She told her daddy what she had seen over the wall.

"That must be Mrs. Bundy's granddaughter," he said. "Let's go meet her."

7

"I can't," Jennifer said, tugging on his hand.

Daddy smiled. "Play with her like you would play with any other little girl," he said.

Jennifer soon found that playing with Kim, Mrs. Bundy's granddaughter, was easy. They dressed their dolls. They made tunnels in the sandbox.

Then Jennifer jumped up and ran across the yard. "Let's swing," she said. Then she stopped. "I forgot. You can't run."

"That's OK," Kim answered. "If your dad helps me on the swing, will you push?"

Up. Back. Up. Back. Creak. Creak. Up. Back.

Jennifer was glad she had found a new friend.

ACTIVITY
Guessing Game

Put a few objects in a paper sack. See if your child can guess what's inside by feeling and not peeking. Does he or she know that vision-impaired persons often use their hands to "see"? Talk about how Jesus was a friend to all kinds of people.

Frienship With a Special-Needs Child

Jesus and Me . . .
On a Rainy Day

José pressed his nose to the window.

"Go away, rain," he said. "I want to go outside and play."

Daddy came into the room. "We could pray about it."

José folded his hands. He squeezed his eyes shut and waited for Daddy to talk.

"Thank You for giving us rain for the flowers and trees," Daddy prayed. "But if it is Your will, please let it stop now. José and I want to play outside again. Amen."

When José opened his eyes, it was still raining. It rained during lunch. It rained at naptime.

"Quick!" Daddy said after José woke up. "Look outside."

It was sunny but still raining. Daddy pointed to the sky.

"Colors!" José said.

"God gave us a rainbow," Daddy told him. "He's reminding us that it won't rain forever."

Then the rain slowed and stopped.

I see yellow.

I see green.

Where do they come from?

What do they mean?

I see red.

I see blue.

God made them

For me and you!

ACTIVITY
Find a Rainbow

You Need: Bathing suits, towels, and a hose or sprinkler.

Cool off today by playing in the hose or sprinkler. With your back to the sun, can you and your child find the "rainbow" in the water?

God Keeps His Promises

Jesus and Me . . .
At the Playground

Danielle climbed into the wagon. Mommy put Ollie, their wriggly puppy, on Danielle's lap.

"Doggy kisses tickle," Danielle said as Ollie licked her knees.

"Here we go," Mommy said.

The wagon bumped, then splashed through a puddle. Finally, they turned a corner and stopped.

Danielle climbed out and ran to the swings. Ollie jumped out and ran after her.

"Up!" Danielle said, patting a swing. Her hand stuck. "Yuck!"

"That is yucky," Mommy said, coming closer. "Old gum!" She picked the gooey mess off with a leaf. Ollie ran to the basketball court. He came back with a dirty paper cup in his mouth.

"That's a good idea, boy," Mommy said. She looked around the playground. "There's a lot of trash here. Jesus would want us to pick it up."

Danielle took the cup from Ollie's mouth and threw it in the trash can by the tree. Mommy picked up paper bags and cans. She picked up newspapers and bottles.

She put the paper bags and newspapers in the trash can. She put the bottles and cans in the wagon. "We can recycle these," she said.

"Is Jesus happy now?" Danielle asked.

"Yes, I'm sure we made Jesus happy," Mommy said. "Now, who wants to play?"

Danielle ran to the swings. Ollie ran after her.

ACTIVITY
Litter Pickup

Choose a safe environment and clean up litter with your child. God made the earth litter free and beautiful. Ask your child how he or she thinks the litter got there.

Taking Care of the Earth

Jesus and Me . . .
And the Special Day

"Wake up, Mommy!" Whitney bounced on her parents' bed holding a picture she and her brother had made. "Happy birthday!"

Mommy rolled over and looked at the picture. "Thank you." She gave Whitney a kiss. "These butterflies are very good."

Whitney didn't tell her they were supposed to be balloons.

"Happy birthday," Daddy told Mommy, when he walked to the front door. "I'm sorry I have to go to work, and I can't be with you all day."

"I know," Mommy said, "but the children are helping to make the day special."

That night, Mommy tucked Whitney into bed.

"Did you have a happy birthday," Whitney asked, "even though Daddy had to work?"

"It was fine," Mommy said. "My three presents made it special."

Whitney scratched her head. "We only gave you one present," she said. "The picture."

"Right," Mommy said, "but God also gave me presents. He gave me you, Chad, and Adam—my children!"

Whitney was glad God had made Mommy happy on her special day. And she was even happier to be one of Mommy's gifts.

Thank You for big people in our lives

Like grandmas, sitters, and others.

Thank You for giving kids families

Like daddies, pets, and mothers. Amen.

ACTIVITY
Blanket Riding

Take a blanket outside in a wide-open area of grass. Have your child sit in the middle of the blanket. Pull on one end of the blanket to give him or her a ride. If there are younger siblings, let the older ones try pulling them. (Babies can lie on their bellies for rides too.)

Children Are Gifts From God

Jesus and Me . . .
At the Jobsite

Willie and his uncle sat in the field behind Willie's house.

Across the dirt road, a muddy truck with a scoop scraped into the ground, making a gigantic hole.

"See over there?" Uncle Rick pointed to a fat, rounded truck. "It's holding cement. They'll dump it in the hole."

"Can we watch that too?" Willie asked.

Uncle Rick stood. "Sorry. I have to go to work. And you can't stay here alone. But your mom or dad might bring you back."

When Willie got home, he begged, "Will you take me back to watch the trucks, Mom? Will you?"

Willie's mother said, "Not now."

"Will you, Daddy, please?" Willie asked.

Willie's dad said, "Not now."

Willie sat on the back porch. He could hear the trucks but couldn't see them.

I could sneak away, Willie thought. *Nobody would know.*

The thought made Willie's tummy jump. Then he remembered that Jesus was with him, even on his back porch. Jesus would know.

I won't sneak away," Willie decided. *I want to do what's right.*

"Hey, sport!" Willie looked up to see his dad. "I can watch the trucks with you now."

"Yippee!" Willie said. He jumped up and tugged his dad's hand. Maybe they could still see the truck dump the cement.

I don't need help for "yeses,"

And "maybes" are OK.

But, Jesus, the "noes"

Are awfully tough!

Please help me to obey.

ACTIVITY
Painting With Water

You Need: Paintbrushes, bucket of water

Your children will have fun "painting" tree trunks, sidewalks, or the house with water. But be sure they understand that it's OK to paint with water only (or you may be in for an unpleasant surprise should they ever get their hands on real paint!).

Doing What's Right

Jesus and Me . . .
Go to Church

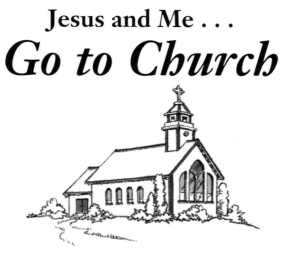

Mallory squirmed, trying to give herself more room. She felt squashed between Mommy and Robbie.

"The seat hurts my knee pits."

"Shhh!" her mother said.

Mallory tried to sit quietly as the preacher talked in big-people language, but soon she felt wiggly again. "Mommy," she said.

"Whisper!" Mommy whispered.

"I'm thirsty," Mallory said a little softer.

"Me too," Robbie added.

"Come." Mommy took their hands. She led them down the aisle.

Mallory liked the drinking fountain in the hall. She stood on tiptoe and turned the cold handle. Water splashed into her mouth and down her chin. She held the handle for Robbie.

"When we go back in, you'll have to sit quietly so the big people can worship God," Mommy said. She dabbed Mallory's wet chin with a tissue. Robbie tilted his chin toward his mother too.

"I'm big," Mallory said. "I want to worship too."

"Me too," Robbie said. "What's worship?"

"One way is to think about things God made," Mommy told them.

"We can do that, right?" Mallory said. Robbie nodded.

"Quietly?" Mommy asked. Mallory scrunched her nose, thinking. Mommy looked at her watch. "For about ten minutes?"

"I'll think of my ten most favorite animals," Mallory decided.

"Me too," Robbie said.

Mommy opened the door, and they walked to their seats quietly. They were worshiping.

> I can make my fingers wiggle (wiggle fingers),
>
> I can make my body jiggle (jiggle body);
>
> But when I pray, you know I will (fold hands)
>
> Sit quietly and be real still (bow head, close eyes).

ACTIVITY
Make a Picture Worship Book

You Need: Construction paper, old magazines, glue stick, scissors, staples or yarn

Help your child find pictures of things God created. He or she can cut them out and glue them on pages of construction paper folded in half. Fasten the pages book style by stapling or tying yarn at the fold. Take the Worship Book with you to worship services to encourage your child to worship too.

Worshiping Is for Children Too

Jesus and Me . . .
At Day Care

Matthew patted the sidewalk.

"That's your shadow," his baby sitter told him. "See mine?"

Her shadow was taller. It stretched from the sidewalk to the front door of the apartment building.

"Who wants to play shadow tag?" she called.

"Me! Me!" the older children shouted.

"Me!" Matthew shouted, even though he didn't know what shadow tag was.

He laughed as the other children ran after the baby sitter's shadow. When the baby sitter ran, the shadow followed her. When she sat, the shadow sat. When she skipped, the shadow skipped.

Matthew lifted a foot. His shadow lifted a foot. He jumped. It jumped. He waved his arms. So did the shadow. He drove his tricycle on the sidewalk. His shadow followed in the grass.

He jumped off and ran behind a tree. Wait! There was no shadow! "Hey, my shadow's gone!"

"It's OK," the sitter said, running to him. "Your shadow will come back. Go into the sunshine again."

Matthew patted his shadow on the sidewalk.

"See? It never went away. You just couldn't see it," the sitter said.

"It's like Jesus," an older boy said. "You can't see Jesus, but He's always with you."

The boy ran to join in a baseball game. Matthew was happy that Jesus was watching him play with his shadow.

Shadows are fun.

They get big and tall.

They also get tiny

Or aren't there at all.

I hide from my shadow

Under the tree,

But I can't run from Jesus,

And He won't run from me.

ACTIVITY
Tracing Shadows

You need: A sunny day, chalk

Let your child make a funny pose. Using chalk, trace his or her shadow onto the sidewalk.

Jesus Is Always With Us

Jesus and Me . . .
And the Chickenpox

Trang looked at the red bumps on her belly.

"I'm sorry," Mommy said. "You have chickenpox."

Daddy felt Trang's head. "You're warm," he said. "Crawl back into bed and rest."

"But, Daddy," Trang said, "what about the picnic?"

Trang's sister Chau started to cry. "Trang will miss all the fun!"

Later that day, Trang hugged a doll her grandmother had sent her from Vietnam. From her bed, she listened to the family getting ready to leave for the picnic.

"How are you feeling?" Daddy asked, coming in to sit by Trang on her bed.

"A little itchy," Trang answered. She liked feeling Daddy's cool hands brush the hair off her face. She had a question for him. "Daddy, why did Chau cry? I'm the one missing the picnic, not her."

"She loves you with the kind of love Jesus has," he said. "She understands how it feels to be sad, and it makes her sad that you're sad."

When Trang was alone, the picture of Jesus on her wall looked blurry through her tears. *Chau is sad for me*, she thought. *Jesus is sad for me too. But I'll get better soon, and they will be happy for me.*

When Jesus was a child of three,

I wonder if He was just like me?

Did He ever itch with pox,

Or skin His knee on slippery rocks?

Did He cry when He was sad?

Was darkness scary? Did He get mad?

Did Jesus like to play in dirt?

Did a blankie take away His hurt?

When Jesus was a child of three,

I think that He was just like me.

ACTIVITY

Lacing a Heart

You Need: Lightweight cardboard, hole punch, yarn, masking tape, marker

Cut a large heart-shape from cardboard. Punch holes around the heart, about 1/4 inch apart and 1/4 inch from the edges. Cut a piece of yarn long enough for sewing. Wrap tape on one end to prevent fraying, and tie the other end to a hole. Now your child can "sew" around the heart.

Jesus Loves Us

Jesus and Me . . .
At the Farmers' Market

Click, clack, click, clack went the wheels of the stroller. Aaron watched colors fly by. Red raspberries. Green peas. Purple grapes.

Click, clack, click, clack. Yellow lemons. Orange carrots. Brown onions.

"Oh no!" someone cried.

"What a mess!" Mother said. "We'd better help."

They moved closer to spilled apples and puddles of cider.

"That truck backed up too far," a woman cried. "My stand is ruined!"

"Don't worry," Mother told her. "I'll help."

"I'll help," said a man in a straw hat. He mopped the cider.

Mother and the woman picked up apples.

The apples looked like they were running away. *I will help catch them too*, Aaron decided.

Aaron climbed out of his stroller. He scooted under the table and picked up yellow and green apples. He grabbed red ones from behind the potato stand.

When the mess was cleaned up, the woman hugged Mother. She

shook the hand of the man in the straw hat. She gave Aaron a shiny red apple. Aaron smiled. Red was his favorite color.

Click, clack, click, clack—CRUNCH! Juice trickled down Aaron's chin.

I'm not a super hero

Who flies to troubled scenes.

I'm just a child of Jesus

Who knows what caring means.

I help when others need me;

I do what I can do.

'Cause when you care about Jesus,

You care for others too.

ACTIVITY
Potato Prints

You Need: Firm fruit or potatoes, knife, teaspoon, paper, tempera paints, plastic lids

Pour paint in lids. Cut fruit or potato in half, and cut around the edges, leaving a shape. Show your child how to dip fruit in the paint and dab it on paper to make designs. Your child can also design shapes by using a metal teaspoon for "cutting." Maybe your child wants to make a picture full of green, red, and yellow "runaway" apples.

Being Considerate

Jesus and Me . . .
And My Garden

Christopher peeked under a bushy plant.

"Another zucchini," he called.

Mommy walked across the lawn to Christopher. "We've had zucchini muffins. We've had zippy zucchini casserole. We've had tomato-zucchini stir-fry," she said. "What else can we do with zucchini?"

Christopher thought of a new plan for zucchini. He explained it to Mommy during lunch.

"Great idea!" she said.

That evening, Daddy, Mommy, and Christopher walked across the field to the town houses.

"You may ring the doorbell," Daddy told Christopher at a doorstep.

They waited a long time. Then an old man slowly opened the door.

Christopher handed him a bulky bag.

"Christopher wanted you to have these," Mommy told the man.

"Since you don't have a garden of your own."

The man looked inside. A smile wrinkled his face. "Thank you. I love zucchini."

Christopher's face wrinkled into a smile too.

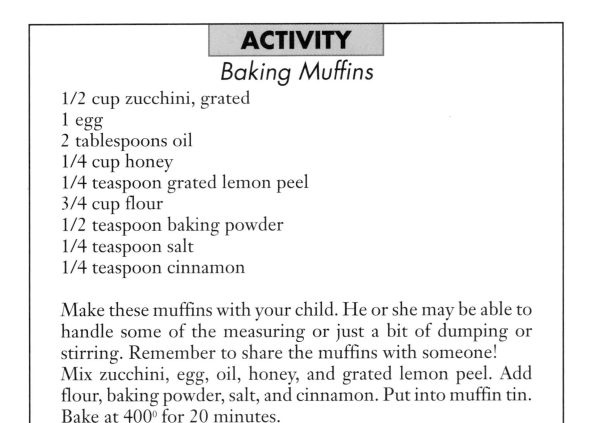

ACTIVITY
Baking Muffins

1/2 cup zucchini, grated
1 egg
2 tablespoons oil
1/4 cup honey
1/4 teaspoon grated lemon peel
3/4 cup flour
1/2 teaspoon baking powder
1/4 teaspoon salt
1/4 teaspoon cinnamon

Make these muffins with your child. He or she may be able to handle some of the measuring or just a bit of dumping or stirring. Remember to share the muffins with someone!
Mix zucchini, egg, oil, honey, and grated lemon peel. Add flour, baking powder, salt, and cinnamon. Put into muffin tin. Bake at 400° for 20 minutes.

Giving to Others

When I'm Sorry

"I'm thirsty," Enju said.

"Enju!" Mother shrieked. She caught the milk jug before it fell to the floor. "I'll help you when I'm through shelling peas."

Mother shelled pea pods. Bright green peas dropped into a pan. Then she started slicing tomatoes.

"I'm thirsty," Enju said again. Her mother didn't seem to hear her.

Enju took her favorite cup from the sink. She tipped the milk carton. *Glug, glug, glug* went the milk. The cup toppled over. *Glug, glug, glug.* The milk wouldn't stop.

"No!" Mother grabbed the jug. She set it on the table with a thud. "How could you!"

Enju ran upstairs to her room. She hid in her closet, behind a box of old baby clothes. She grabbed her teddy bear and hugged it. Tears soaked the bear's ribbon.

Mommy said she would help me, she told him angrily. *I have the meanest mother in the world.*

There was a knock on her door. Enju watched her mother from behind the box.

"I'm sorry I didn't pour your milk when I said I would." Mother looked under the bed. "I was wrong to be angry."

Enju came out of the closet. "I'm sorry too," she said quietly. "Do you still hate me?"

"Hate you!" Mother said. She tilted Enju's chin upward and looked into her eyes. "I was upset that you didn't obey. So was Jesus. But just like Jesus, I'll never stop loving you."

I'm in the closet

Behind the box.

Nobody sees me here—

Not Daddy or Mommy or

Anyone else

'Cept Jesus . . . and my teddy bear.

ACTIVITY
Musical Hide-and-Seek

You Need: A music box or musical stuffed toy

Wind up and hide the music box or toy, and let your child try to find it before it stops playing. Tell older children if they're getting "hotter" or "colder" as they look.
Talk about how we can't hide from God.

Asking Forgiveness

Jesus and Me . . .
At the Beach

"Mine!" André pulled his shovel away from the boy with the alligators on his bathing suit.

Sand flew into the boy's face. André put the shovel behind his back.

"No, no!" André's mother said, jumping up from her beach chair.

"What's wrong?" the other boy's mother asked. She brushed tears and sand from her son's cheeks.

"*My* shovel," André said. He stepped back in the soft sand.

The boy with the alligator suit cried too loudly. André plugged his ears shut with his fingers.

"You've made your new friend sad," Mother said. "What can you do to make him happy again?"

André took his fingers out of his ears. "I want to share," he said. He found a yellow shovel in the beach bag and gave it to the boy.

The boy stopped crying. Together, they dug big holes and little holes. The alligator-suit boy got a bucket from his beach towel. He filled the bucket with water. They took turns dumping the water into the holes.

André's mother looked up from her book. "You're sharing much better now," she said.

André dumped the water on his new friend's knees. Sharing was fun.

When I share my toys with friends,

We all have much more fun.

God shares too—important things

Like Jesus Christ, His Son!

ACTIVITY
Create a Sand Painting

You Need: 1/2 cup clean sand or salt, 1 to 3 tablespoons dry tempera paint or few drops food coloring, shaker bottle, heavy paper

Color sand or salt by mixing the first two ingredients. Your child can "draw" a picture by squeezing white glue on paper. Sprinkle "sand" over the glue. Let dry. Shake off excess.

Sharing

Jesus and Me . . .
Watch the Firefighters

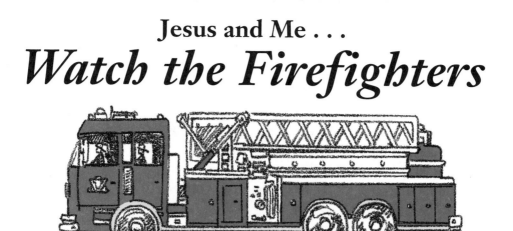

The firetruck screamed down the street. Scott ran to the window to see where it was going.

Amy followed him. "I don't smell smoke."

"The truck stopped at the end of the block," Mother said.

"Can we go watch?" Amy asked. She jumped with excitement but stopped when she saw Mother's worried look.

"Firetrucks mean that someone's in trouble," Mother said.

They watched neighbors rush down the street. Boys whizzed by on their bikes.

It's exciting to us, Amy thought. *But it must be scary for the people in trouble.*

"Let's pray for the people in trouble," she said. Mother nodded. "Dear Jesus, help the firefighters know what to do."

"Jesus," Mother prayed. "Calm the spirits of the people who are in trouble. Let them know You care."

"Amen," Scott added. That was his favorite part.

They walked out to the sidewalk. The firefighters were pulling a hose across the Marinis' front lawn.

"It's not a fire," Mrs. Marini called from her porch. "An old pipe broke in our basement. There's water everywhere."

Mother talked to Mrs. Marini. Scott and Amy watched hoses pump water into tanks.

"I'm going to be a firefighter when I grow up," Scott said.

The firefighter by the truck took off her helmet. Wet curls fell to her shoulders.

"I'm going to be a firefighter too," Amy said. "So I can help people in trouble."

Jesus knows the what and why,

He knows the where and how.

All I know is a siren's screaming,

So I should pray right now.

ACTIVITY
Practice Fire Safety

Practice "stop, drop, and roll," a technique your child should know if he or she ever catches on fire. Also practice crawling (backward when you go down steps) the way he or she would exit a smoke-filled house. Have a fire drill. Does everyone in the family know the designated spot to meet, such as the mailbox?

Pray for People in Trouble

Jesus and Me . . .
And the New Baby

"If the baby has to go to the park, I'm not going!" Reggie crossed his arms and plopped down on the couch.

Mother stopped making faces at the baby. She sat next to Reggie.

"Are you a little green with envy?" she asked.

"I'm not green," Reggie grumbled. "I'm mad." He checked his arms anyway, to be sure they were still brown.

"Saying you're green is another way to say you're jealous," Mother said. "Jesus can help you take that feeling away."

"Can He just take the baby away instead?" Reggie asked, feeling hopeful.

But Mother shook her head.

"Jesus planned for our family," she told him. "Daddy, me, you, your brothers, *and* the new baby."

The baby squealed. Reggie walked across the room and looked in at her. She grabbed his finger and stopped crying.

"She likes me!" he said.

"Of course," Mother answered. "You're her big brother."

"I don't want to be green anymore," Reggie said. "I'll ask Jesus to take it away. Then we can show the baby the park where she'll play when she's big like me."

On weekends, Lisa sees her dad.

Brett stays with his mother.

Allison lives with a dad and mom,

Five sisters, and a brother.

Jessica's brother's a baby,

Mine is older than me.

But Jesus planned for all of us

To live as families.

ACTIVITY
Pretend Parenting

You Need: Baby dolls; dishpan of water, soap, shampoo, washcloths and towels

Wash the dolls outside, where spills and splashes just add to the fun. Talk about special circumstances in your family. Are there also sibling-rivalry issues that you could talk about?

Overcoming Jealousy

Jesus and Me . . .
At the Doctor

Dr. Jones put a cold circle on Kate's chest. "Take a big breath." He put the circle on Kate's back. "Another big breath."

Kate thought it was fun to be up high on the table. She liked watching Dr. Jones. She wondered what Dr. Jones would do next.

"Are you getting plenty of exercise in the fresh air?" Dr. Jones asked.

Kate nodded.

"Open wide and say 'ahhh,'" the doctor said.

Kate opened her mouth. Dr. Jones shone a light inside and looked at Kate's throat.

"Are you eating healthy foods?" Dr. Jones asked. "Lots of veggies and fruit?"

Kate nodded.

"Drinking lots of water each day?" Dr. Jones asked.

Kate nodded again.

"Taking naps and going to bed without fussing?" Dr. Jones raised his eyebrows and smiled. He looked at Kate's mother across the room.

"She does fairly well," Mother said, smiling.

Dr. Jones patted Kate's knee and helped Kate jump down from the table.

"My legs are strong too," Kate said.

"Yes, they are," the doctor said. He handed Mother a paper. He handed Kate a sticker of a hot-air balloon.

"You're taking good care of the body God gave you," Dr. Jones said to Kate. "Everything looks good."

My arms are for hugging (hug self).

My button's for fun (poke belly).

God gave me my legs (run in place) so I can run.

My ears are for hearing (tug ears).

My eyes can blink (blink).

God gave me a brain (point to head) so I can think.

ACTIVITY

Give directions to your child such as "point to your nose, now your toes . . ." Does your child know the trickier parts, such as wrist, waist, and hips? Challenge older preschoolers with harder directions. (Put your right hand on your head. Touch your elbow to your knee.)

We Care for Our Bodies

Jesus and Me . . .
And My Swimming Lesson

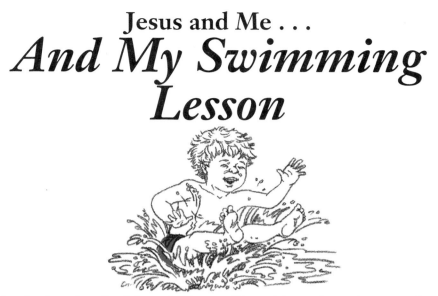

"Today's the day," chimed Tracy, Derek's swimming teacher. Her eyes looked sky blue, like the pool. "I'll be right here to catch you."

Geoffrey was in the deeper water, tossing a ball to a boy from the neighborhood. Derek needed more lessons from Tracy before it would be safe for him to join them, but it looked like fun.

"One . . ." Tracy said.

Derek stepped back and shook his head. His knees felt wobbly.

"Two . . ." Tracy said. She held out her arms.

What if Tracy misses me and I sink to the bottom? Derek worried.

"Three!" Tracy said. "You can do it!"

"I want to do it, Jesus," Derek prayed. He stepped forward, two tiny steps, then a leap! *Kersplash!* He held his breath and hit the water.

Tracy reached for him. Derek giggled and kicked to the side of the pool, the way Tracy taught him. His breath came out in short puffs. "I did it!"

"You sure did!" Tracy helped him crawl out. "Try it again."

See me, Jesus?

Watch me!

I swim and kick my feet.

See me, Jesus?

Watch me!

The things I do are neat!

See me, Jesus?

Watch me!

I blow bubbles,

Blub, blub, blub.

See me, Jesus?

Watch me!

I'm swimming—in the tub!

ACTIVITY
Water Play

You Need: Bathtub or wading pool, cups, squeeze bottles, spray bottles, funnel

Encourage "measuring," splashing, and squirting. Ask your child if he or she thinks specific objects will sink or float. Let him or her test them.

Overcoming Jealousy

Jesus and Me . . .
On Our Vacation

Emily pressed her nose against the car window. It didn't look like the city anymore. She saw trees fly past. She saw cows and horses in fields. "Are we there yet?"

"We're in the country," Mommy said. "We have a long way to go." Mommy read Emily a story about farm animals.

Emily looked out the window. She saw empty sidewalks and small stores. She saw street lights and stop signs. "Are we there yet?"

"We're in a small town," Daddy said. "We have a long way to go."

Emily made funny faces at David. Then he fell asleep. The car stopped. "Are we there?"

"This is a toll booth," Mommy said. She dug a coin from her purse. Daddy tossed it out his window into a basket. "We have to pay to drive across this bridge."

The car started again. Emily put her head on David's car seat. The car's motor hummed her to sleep.

"Wake up!" Mommy said, shaking Emily's shoulder. "We're here."

The car stopped. Emily got out of the car and stretched.

"There's the ocean, see?" Emily followed Mommy's pointing finger. She had never seen so much water before. It looked scary.

Emily hid her face in Mommy's skirt. "Let's go home."

She felt Daddy lift her. "Jesus was with us in the city, Emily," he said. His words were warm against her neck. "Jesus was with us in the country and the town. He was with us the whole time we traveled. And He will be with us here too."

Emily felt safe enough to look at the water again.

Jesus is in the city

And in the country too.

He stops and goes when you do

And never loses you!

ACTIVITY
Car Game

Say "I see something red [or other color]." Your child can make as many guesses as necessary until he or she guesses the object you have in mind.

For younger children, give a more in-depth description. After each wrong guess, add another detail until he or she guesses it or you reveal the answer.

This can be played on long or short trips or as you wait for appointments in public places.

Jesus Is With You When You Travel

Jesus and Me . . .
On a Treasure Hunt

Taylor picked up a bright green leaf. He put it in his shoe box. "This is a funny treasure hunt. I thought we would find coins and jewels."

"Coins and jewels are people treasures," Mother said. She placed an acorn in Taylor's box. "We're looking for treasures from God."

"A caterpillar!" Taylor said. He tried to pluck the fuzzy creature off a stick. It rolled into a ball and fell to the ground.

"Let it go," Mother said. "We don't want to hurt it."

Why do I have to be careful? Taylor wondered. *It's just a bug.* He watched the caterpillar stretch out and inch toward the bush again. It crawled back to the stick.

"The caterpillar's more than a bug," he remembered out loud. "It's a treasure from God too."

Mother looked under a petunia plant in her garden. "Come quick!" she said. "Here's another treasure."

Lions and walruses are neat in the zoo,

But here in my yard, I like to see you!

Lying on my belly, I can watch you for hours,

Busily working out here near the flowers.

I like your home under my mom's plants.

Aren't you glad God made you, ants?

ACTIVITY
Treasure Hunt/Leaf Rubbings

You Need: Paper bag or shoe box for collecting things, green leaves, scotch tape, typing paper, crayons with paper removed

Search for "treasures from God" with your child, reminding him or her which treasures are all right to collect and which ones are happier just being watched.
To make a leaf rubbing, tape a leaf, ribbings side up, to a table. Place white paper over it. Let your child rub the paper with the side of a crayon. The leaf will appear. Try a variety of leaves.

Caring for God's Creation

Jesus and Me . . .
In the Kitchen

Jacquelyn's mother was mowing. Her brother John trimmed along the driveway. Jacquelyn found her dad in the kitchen. He chopped mushrooms and dropped them in a skillet. He snapped broccoli from bunches. He tossed them in the skillet too. The vegetables sizzled and spit.

Then he noticed Jacquelyn watching him. "Why the sad face?" he asked.

"I'm too little to mow," Jacquelyn said. "I'm too little to trim. I'm too little to cook. I can't do anything."

Dad cracked three eggs, letting the goo run into a bowl.

Jacquelyn wondered if he had been listening to her. Then he handed her a whisk.

"You can whip the eggs," he said.

She whipped them until her arm ached and the eggs were foamy, like a bubble bath.

"You're the best whipper in town," Dad said. "Jesus is happy when you do a good job."

Jacquelyn felt happy too. She had found a way to help.

43

THE HELPING SONG

(To the tune of "Here We Go 'Round the Mulberry Bush")

This is a way that I can help, I can help, I can help.

This is a way that I can help. I can _____.

(Fill in with ways your child can help in your home, church,

neighborhood, and at day care.)

ACTIVITY
Make Pretend Food

You Need: Store-bought Play-Doh or recipe below
3 cups flour
1 cup salt
1 cup water
few drops food coloring
safe kitchen tools, such as a plastic knife, rolling pin, wooden
spoons, gadgets

Mix all ingredients, if making your own no-cook dough. (It
takes a lot of kneading, which your child can help with.) Your
child will have fun making and serving the Play-Doh food to
all your family members. Be sure siblings know it shouldn't
be eaten! Set a table, and serve favorite dolls or stuffed animals
too.

Being a Helper

Jesus and Me . . .
On My Birthday

"Wake up!" Melina bounced on the side of the bed.

"It's early," Mommy said, rubbing her eyes. Daddy groaned.

"Wake up," Melina said again. "It's my birthday! I'm three!"

"Lie down with us." Mommy patted the space between Daddy and her. Melina crawled in.

"Was it three years ago already that God gave us that tiny baby girl?" Mommy said in a sleepy voice.

"A crying, wetting, wrinkly baby girl," Daddy said, grinning. He sat up against his pillow. "You were no bigger than a peanut!"

"You're teasing," Melina said.

"Only about the peanut part," he answered. "Now look at you. You're so big, there's no room for me in the bed."

He yelped for help and pretended to be pushed off the bed.

Melina giggled and reached for him. He scooped her into his arms.

"Happy birthday, Peanut," he said.

"I'm three," Melina said. "Happy birthday to me!"

Count the candles (child holds up three fingers),

One, two, three (point to one for each number).

Jesus, are You watching me?

Next year, see me get one more (child holds up

another finger),

One, two, three (point to each),

And one more—four (point to fourth finger)!

ACTIVITY

Celebrate Birth/Make Hand Prints

You Need: Tempera or finger paints, plastic lids, paper

Look at photos of your child's birth and infancy. Talk about growth and changes over the years. Tell your child about preparing for him or her and who you called to tell of the birth. Celebrate your child's birth together!

Put small amounts of paint in plastic lids, large enough for your child's hand. Press his or her hand on the paint. You may need to rub the paint on each finger to be sure it's even. Make hand prints on the paper. Name and date the paper to compare growth over the years!

Physical Growth

Jesus and Me . . .
In My Backyard

Jenny pedaled her big-wheeled trike to the bottom of the driveway.

"Stop right there," a voice demanded.

Troy, the meanest boy in the neighborhood, pointed a toy laser gun at her.

Jenny didn't like guns. Even toy ones. She was about to run into the house the way she had done the day before.

"Jesus wants you to be nice to him," the baby sitter had told her. "Troy will probably be nicer to you too."

Jenny hopped off her big wheel. "I have a trampoline in my backyard," she said. "Want to jump on it?"

Troy dropped the gun. "Race you," he said.

Jenny ran as fast as she could. She beat Troy to the trampoline. He pushed ahead of her and climbed up.

The sitter waved at her from the kitchen window.

"We can take turns," Jenny told Troy. "I'll go next."

"*Boing! Boing!*" Troy said, jumping into the air. He didn't look as mean when he was smiling.

47

Be Kind (An Action Poem)

Be kind, be kind, be kind to one another.
The Bible tells us to be kind (hug your friend).

Be a friend, be a friend, be good friends to one another.
Jesus shows us in the Bible, be a friend (shake hands with your friend).

Share a smile, share a smile, share a smile with each other.
God wants you to be happy; share a smile (smile at friend).

Be a friend, be a friend, be good friends to one another.
If you're friends to one another, shout "Amen" (shout "Amen!").

ACTIVITY
Making a Kazoo

You Need: A clean comb, wax paper

Make a kazoo by loosely covering the comb with wax paper.

Tell your child to say "hum" while his or her lips are on the paper. Make up a tune to the poem, singing while your child plays the instrument.

Being Kind to Someone Unkind

Jesus and Me . . .
At Naptime

"I'm not sleepy!" Leeza wiped a hot tear from her cheek. She ran behind the sofa. "No nap!"

"Leeza!" her mother said. "I'm going to count to three. One, two . . ." Leeza crawled out from behind the sofa.

"You're so tired," Mommy said. When she picked her up, Leeza put her head on Mommy's shoulder. It was hard to keep her eyes open.

Mommy carried her up the steps. Leeza heard her sisters playing in the other bedroom. She heard her brothers in the backyard. Leeza lifted her head.

"I'm not sleepy!" she said again. "No nap!"

"You'll be happier when you wake up." Mommy lowered Leeza to her bed. She turned the fan on her. She handed her Mr. Bunny with the hole in his ear.

Leeza closed her eyes and listened to Mommy pray.

"Dear Jesus, please help Leeza get the rest she needs."

The pillow was soft and comfy. Air blew gently on Leeza's face. And Mr. Bunny, with the hole in his ear, snuggled against her neck.

Jesus was helping Leeza get the rest she needed.

Little Ms. Leeza

Doesn't want to go to bed.

Little Ms. Leeza

Thinks she should play instead.

Little Ms. Leeza,

You're miserable as can be.

Little Ms. Leeza,

You need rest like me!

ACTIVITY
Making Naptime Tapes

Read Bible or other favorite stories into a tape recorder. Your child can participate by making sounds to correspond with the words (such as a "moo" every time a cow is mentioned) or by saying repeated lines. Play the tape at naptime or when a parenting break is needed!

The Body Needs Rest

Jesus and Me . . .
Watch the Sky

"That one looks like a lamb," Benny said.

Trevor nodded. "It's next to the dragon stuck in a tree."

"Good imaginations," Mother said. "Guess what I see in the clouds."

"A lamb?" Benny asked.

"Not a lamb," Mother said.

"A dragon in a tree?" Trevor asked.

"Not a dragon in a tree," his mother answered. "I'm using my imagination to see Jesus coming back with the clouds. I can almost hear a great trumpet and see His people rushing forward to Him!"

Trevor jumped up. "I have a picture of that in my Bible!"

Benny popped up too. "Could it happen today?"

Mother patted the boys' blanket. They both lay down again.

"Nobody knows when," Mother said. "But the Bible promises us it will happen. God wants us to imagine it."

Trevor looked up. He wasn't imagining a dragon stuck in a tree. He wasn't thinking about the lamb in the sky. Those things were just pretend. He was thinking about Jesus. He thought, *Someday, I'll really see Him.*

> Except for pretend, I'll never see
>
> A silly old dragon, stuck up in a tree.
>
> But someday I will see Jesus' smiling face,
>
> And He'll take me to His heavenly place.

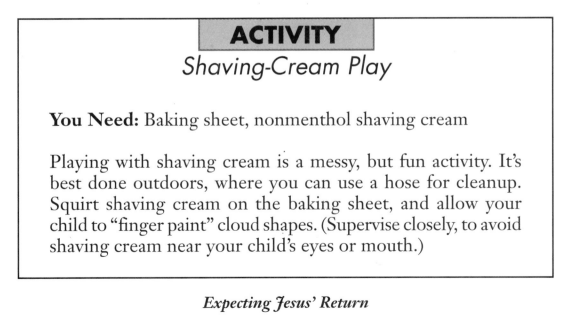

ACTIVITY
Shaving-Cream Play

You Need: Baking sheet, nonmenthol shaving cream

Playing with shaving cream is a messy, but fun activity. It's best done outdoors, where you can use a hose for cleanup. Squirt shaving cream on the baking sheet, and allow your child to "finger paint" cloud shapes. (Supervise closely, to avoid shaving cream near your child's eyes or mouth.)

Expecting Jesus' Return

Jesus and Me . . .
When I'm Five

Thump, thump thump.

"Go away," came the answer from the other side of the door.

Sally knocked again.

"I'm reading!" her sister Emily shouted this time. Sally found Luis in the family room. He was reading a magazine. She found her father in his office reading the newspaper. She tried to climb on his lap.

"Not now, Sally," Father said. "I want to finish the sports page."

Clark was in the dining room. He was gluing the wing on a model airplane. He read the directions from a wrinkled paper next to the pieces.

Mother carried a laundry basket up the stairs.

"What's wrong?" she asked.

"Everybody can read but me," Sally answered.

Mother set the basket down.

"Look at my face," she said. "Can you read how I'm feeling?"

Sally laughed at her mother's silly smile.

"You're happy," she said.

Mother made her bottom lip droop.

"You're sad," Sally said.

Mother kissed Sally on the head. "God has a perfect time for everything. You aren't ready to read words yet. But you're a good reader of faces."

Someday I'll learn how to climb trees;

I won't cry when I hear buzzing bees.

I'll use the toilet; I'll wash my own face;

I'll put my toys away, neatly in place.

I might have a bike, a two-wheeler, I think;

I won't need a stool for reaching the sink.

But for now . . . Jesus, help me to grow,

And keep me patient when it feels too slow.

ACTIVITY
Storytelling

Make up a story by taking turns saying a few lines. This can be done with just the two of you, or include other family members.

God's Timing Is Perfect

Jesus and Me . . .
At the Park

Justin climbed the ladder of the sliding board. Up, up, up. Then he slipped down. It made his belly tickle.

"Hey, Grandpa," he said at the bottom. "Look!" He pointed.

A bird sat on a picnic table.

"Shh! Don't scare the little guy," Grandpa said, moving closer.

"He's shiny," Justin whispered.

"He's so black he almost looks blue," Grandpa whispered back. "When we get home, I'll look up his name in my bird book."

"His name should be Ralph," Justin said. He forgot to whisper. The bird flew. If Justin leaned way back, he could still see the bird on the top of a tree.

"Ralph?" Grandpa said, smiling. He rubbed the top of Justin's head. "Maybe. Aren't you glad Jesus made Ralph for us to enjoy? Let's go see if Ralph is a purple martin or a grackle."

Justin liked feeling his hand in Grandpa's as they walked home.

From the picnic table

To the top of a tree,

Jesus sees the black bird

Just like me.

ACTIVITY

Make a Bird-feeder Garland/Name the Birds

You Need: A bird book (from the library), string or heavy thread, chunks of fruit, popped popcorn, *O*-shaped cereal, raisins, blunt-end needle

Look through a bird book with your youngster. Can he or she find a bird the same color as the one in the story? What kind is it?
Double-thread and knot a blunt-end needle. Let your child string the ingredients above in any order. Hang on a tree by a window for bird-watching.

Appreciating God's Creation

Jesus and Me . . .
When I'm Sick

David needed his tonsils out. He went to the hospital.

"Slip on this gown, honey," a nurse told him. He hated the gown. It looked like a women's nightie.

Mommy prayed aloud. "Jesus, help David be a good patient."

Later, David woke up in a strange bed. Now, he was wearing the funny women's nightie, and his throat hurt. He was almost afraid, but then he saw his mother.

"The operation is over," Mommy said. "You will soon be fine." She handed him a colorful card. "This is from the children at church. And look what Daddy brought you from home."

David reached for his favorite teddy bear. His throat still hurt, but his insides felt happier.

Mommy prayed aloud. "Thank You, Jesus, for helping David to be a good patient. And thank You for David's friends."

My tummy's turning upside down;
The thermometer pokes my tongue.
I'm hot with covers, cold without;
I want this sickness done!

But Mommy's hands are cool and nice;
My sister reads to me.
Cards and pictures come in the mail,
Which I can't wait to see.

Thank You, Jesus, for Mommy's hands,
For a sister who can read,
And friends who cared enough today
To mail nice things to me.

ACTIVITY

Making Greeting Cards

You Need: Construction paper, watered-down tempera paints, drinking straw, pen

Put one teaspoon paint in the middle of a paper. Give your child a straw, and tell him or her to blow the paint to make a design. Let dry. Fold in half, and write a get-well message inside.

We Comfort Each Other

Jesus and Me . . .
And the Bible

Allison's lips moved, but no words came out.

Alex giggled at his big sister. "What are you doing?" he asked.

"Trying to memorize a Bible verse," she said. " 'Surely the Sovereign Lord does nothing without . . .' I forgot the last line again!"

" '. . . revealing his plan to his servants the prophets' "! Dad called from the next room.

"Right. 'Surely the Sovereign Lord does nothing without revealing his plan to his servants the prophets.' Amos 3:7 [NIV]."

"That verse is too hard," Alex said. "I could never learn it."

"Some verses are easier," Allison told him. "For little kids."

Alex ran to find his dad. He wanted an easier verse so he could memorize too.

"Let's try this one," Dad said. " 'God is love.' 1 John 4:8."

My Bible is a special Book

Filled with treasures inside.

Memory keeps them in my head

Till they slip to my heart and hide.

ACTIVITY

Memorize a Verse/Make Bible Bookmarkers

You Need: Bible, strips of construction paper, markers

"Thy word I have treasured in my heart." Psalm 119:11, NASB.

Show your child this verse in the Bible. Help him or her memorize it.

Let him or her decorate bookmarks for every member of your family to use in their Bibles. If your child wants, print the words of a verse on each one.

It's Good to Memorize Scripture

Jesus and Me . . .
In the Woods

"What will we do when it gets dark?" Jordan asked.

"We have a lantern," Daddy said.

"And flashlights," Mommy added.

Jordan wasn't sure about sleeping in the woods at night. Even with a lantern. Even with flashlights.

"I think we should go home to sleep," he said.

"Jesus will watch over you," Daddy said. "And Mommy and I will be nearby. Don't worry."

Daddy tossed the sleeping bags into the tents. Jordan unrolled them.

"Do bears come out at night?" he asked.

"There are no bears in these woods," Daddy answered. "Besides, Jesus will watch over you. And Mommy and I will be nearby. Don't worry."

At the creek, Jordan and his parents caught minnows with paper cups. They let them go. They cooked supper on a fire made of wood. Jordan forgot about being afraid until it was time for bed.

"Dear Jesus," Daddy prayed. Jordan snuggled into his sleeping bag. "Watch over Jordan and keep him safe all night long. Amen."

Zip! Daddy shut the flap. Jordan was alone in the dark tent.

There's nothing to worry about, he remembered Daddy saying. *Jesus is watching over you. And Mommy and Daddy are close by.*

"Good night, Jesus," he said. Then Jordan fell asleep.

My night light is glowing;

I hold Teddy tight.

It must be time to say good night.

Good night, Jesus.

ACTIVITY
Pretend Camping

You Need: Small tent or blankets to make one

A toddler may enjoy just going in and out of the tent, playing peekaboo with you. Or pad the ground with sleeping bags for naptime, lunch, or a comfy spot to discuss your child's fears. Make a pretend fire with sticks. Use a flashlight or other camping gear you may have.

Protection in the Dark